AF413511

SELL LIFE INSURANCE PROUDLY

51 SECRET SALES IDEAS, PITCHES, STORIES, ACTIVITIES ON SELLING LIFE INSURANCE

HARBANS LAL ARORA

Made with ♥ on the Notion Press Platform
www.notionpress.com

Contents

Contents

Contents

Foreword

<u>Ayan Chatterjee</u>
SVP and Head Sales Training - Institution Business.
Bajaj Allianz Life Insurance Company Ltd.

I have known Harbans for last 15 years and in these 15 years, the one thing that has not changed in Harbans is his story telling nature. I have seen him explaining complex problems and situations and make them look so easy, by use of right stories.

I had gone through Harbans's first book " Fail the failure" and I must admit that each story was an eye opener for me.

The concept of introducing an unknown concept through a known story is one of the popular training methodology and Harbans is a master in the same.

In this book, you will be able to experience 51 sales ideas, pitches, stories and activities. These are exclusively for life insurance professionals which will equip them to sell proudly and easily.

I have already experienced the impact of a few of such sales ideas / pitches / stories etc.

While I eagerly look forward to read each of the 51 stories in this book, here is my best wishes to Harbans for all the success.

Keep writing my friend and keep inspiring us.

Preface

You may go to various food outlets across India and world. Have you observed that in every city, there are few famous food outlets where people go again and again and don't mind to wait in queue as well? What makes these food outlets so special, do these outlets order special raw material from some hidden places?

Hey, you know the answer! Everybody can arrange same or better raw material but it's the recipe of food which people share to their next generations in a secret way. Same way, every profession has its **secret recipe** including life insurance. Sellers learnt it in a very hard way. This book is an effort to consolidate those secret recipes and pass it to the next generations. This book is **a culmination of experience of such extraordinary life insurance sellers across world** which made a difference in the lives of Crores of people.

I found that every successful seller has some unique sales ideas / sales pitches / stories / activities which provided good results to the seller however it may / may not work well for others. It is advisable that you pick up a few sales ideas / sales pitches / stories / activities, experiment it with a few of the prospects and then continue with those ideas / pitches / stories / activities which looks natural to you and gives you more closures than others.

Do remember what works today does not mean that it will work forever. Keep reinventing yourself.

Keep challenging yourself and set higher standards for self like Better Conversion Ratio, Higher Case Size, Higher Case Rate, Better productivity, Better Commissions, Better Number of policies, Better Premium, More References, Lesser expenses, Lesser number of hours spent on work, Lesser Lapses, Lesser Claims etc.

Purpose of selecting your own unique sales idea / sales pitch / story / activity is that it ensures uniqueness, undivided attention from prospect and puts you many steps ahead then the crowd of other ordinary sellers.

These techniques can work online or / and offline. You can modify it as per the requirement. Timing of these depends on person to person and situation to situations. Many of them can be used as conversation starters which mean you begin your interaction with these pitches; many of them can be used in between, many of them during closing or objection handling. You are free to experiment with them at different times for different prospects.

<u>Purpose of writing this book is to:</u>

- Life insurance sellers can sell life insurance proudly
- Spread awareness on the importance of life insurance
- Remove various myths associated with it and the sellers
- Die empty (learnings to be transferred to the next generation)
- Life insurance sellers should get the same respect in the society like other professionals

You can start reading this book from anywhere.

Power phrases are given at the end of every chapter. These power phrases can be used as conversation starters; to create interest; to create need; to disturb the emotions, to close the call or handle objections etc. Usage of power phrases depends on situation, customer, and your expertise to use it.

Attempt 8-10 power phrases and use those 4-5 power phrases frequently which gives you more results and looks natural on you. You can keep changing it till you find the most suitable one.

It's your conviction, which gets transfer to your prospect. Do remember that it's not important, what you say but it's more important how you say along with your body language

Acknowledgements

I would like to specially mention the name of **Jyoti Arora** who is better half in every sense and true inspiration behind writing this book. She stood like a wall in every up and down of life. Both daughters – **Khyati Arora** and **Himanya Arora** were partnering in every aspect of life. They are the true back bone behind the launch of this book.

I would like to say a special thanks to all my supervisors, colleagues, team members, trainers, advisors, leaders, clients and other stakeholders for their contribution in my life.

My sincere thanks to all those people who shared these sales ideas / sales pitches / stories / activities through social media, public meetings, through books, articles or through training programs. Few of these ideas are invented by me and few are modified versions.

I acknowledge the contribution of **Ayan Chatterjee** for writing **foreword** of this book.

Sales Ideas / Sales Pitches

Sales ideas / sales pitches are the unique ways adopted by the sellers to sell life insurance.

This can be analogy, anecdotes, examples, ways of explanation etc. so that prospects can relate with life insurance easily.

We are sharing few wonderful sales ideas / sales pitches which proved highly successful for thousands of sellers and helped them to generate more quality and profitable business consistently.

Initially, pick up 5 sales ideas / sales pitches and practice it with your near and dear ones. Take feedback and apply top 3 sales ideas / sales pitches with your prospects. You can keep improvising on these ideas / pitches as per your experience with more and more prospects.

Remember, it's the accountability of seller to make prospect aware about the benefits of life insurance. Seller needs to use customised sales ideas / pitches as per the background / understanding of the prospects. You need to learn from the experiences of meeting new prospects as every prospect is different from others and will respond differently. Don't give up, use your presence of mind and be a great sales person.

CHAPTER ONE

Tyres in the Car

You can ask this question online / offline and preferably it should be done as conversation starter however you can also use it during closing if objection comes.

Ask - how many tyres do a normal car have?

Many prospects will say 4, ask them again whether you are sure about the answer. Few may say 5. Listen carefully.

Appreciate those who say 5 by saying that it's the right answer however don't debate with prospects who say 4.

Say - we all know purpose of 4 tyres of the car however what is the purpose of 5th tyre? Why we keep it in the car? Listen to the answer. \

Ask, "Is it happened with you that 1 tyre got puncture of the car / cab you were travelling? What happened after that?" Listen and nod when prospect shares his / her real-life example.

Else **say** - Just imagine that you plan to travel through a car to a city which is 200 kms away from your home for a relative marriage, your family is also travelling with you. Mid way car tyre got puncture.

Situation 1, 5th tyre is there; you change it in 10 minutes and restart your journey and reach your destination. You enjoy all functions of your relative marriage.

Situation 2, 5th tyre is not there, it's late night time; no puncture shop is there, mobile network is not coming that you can call emergency services, you feel unsafe to take lift from unknown people on a highway. You are cursing that why have you not checked about 5th tyre in the beginning of the trip.

When we buy any car, it comes with 5tyres for situations like above and price for 5th tyre is included in the overall cost of the car. None of us say no to this 5th tyre and we pay for it happily.

Say - let's treat this life as car and you as one tyre. Your family is other tyres of the car. What if something happens to you? Whether your family can run the life smoothly if there is no substitute of you?

Say - I offer this 5th tyre to people like you and it's known as insurance which helped many families so far as nobody knows when death (puncture) will happen of main bread earner.

Power Phrase: To have it when you want it, you have to buy it when you don't need it.

CHAPTER TWO

COST OF WAITING / POSTPONING

While you can use this pitch during anytime. It's recommended that you use it when the prospect tries to postpone the decision of buying life insurance.

Show him / her the cost of waiting. Let's take one example:

- Customer age - 44 years
- Gender - Male
- Smoker status - Non-smoker
- Standard life / Sub Standard life / Health status: Standard life with no health history / risk
- Type of plan - Pure term plan without any rider, without return of premium option
- Sum assured - Rs 1 crore
- Policy term - 40 years
- Premium paying term - 40 years

If the same customer postpones the decision to buy this term plan by 1 year then implications will be as follows (Create a table like this). These rates are just dummy rates for example purpose only. You need to take actual premium rates as per the plan offered by you.

If you decide today

Annual Premium - Rs 40,000

Total Premium for full term - Rs 16,00,000

If you decide after 1 year

Annual Premium - Rs 45,000

Total Premium for full term - Rs 18,00,000

Extra premium paid for one year - Rs 5,000

Extra premium paid for full term - Rs 2,00,000

Tax implications for full term at 18% - Rs 36,000

Total loss for postponement of decision - Rs 2,36,000

Highlight the total loss amount for the full term and it's impact on the goal. Mention that health status can change in future and it can lead to extra loading on the premiums.

In the similar way, keep few examples ready with you for endowment plans, guaranteed plans, ULIP plans, annuity plans etc. Show the loss or its impact on the maturity / goals etc.

Say - the best time to buy a policy is today as you can't go back in past and change it while future is uncertain so let's decide it now.

Power Phrase: Whatever excuse you may have for not buying life insurance now will only sound ridiculous to your widow.

CHAPTER THREE

BENEFITS VERSUS FEATURE

There is one thing common amongst all of us. There is a seller hidden in each one of us whether we accept it or not.

I struggled a lot in sales till the moment I learnt a technique. Let me share that technique which helped me and can be beneficial for you as well.

It is FHB (F-Feature, H-How it works, B-Benefits)
Or

FAB (F-Feature, A-Advantage, B-Benefits).

Both are the same things. Use this technique after doing basic need analysis.

Pick up any top 3 features which are best suitable for the prospect's needs e.g. if you are selling a life insurance product, One of the Feature is, "Limited Premium Paying Term (PPT)".

How it works / Advantage: While the policy term for this plan is 30 years however prospects need not to pay for the full policy term but can pay only for 10 years only.

Benefits:

1. Policy benefits continue for the full policy term of 30 years

2. Peace of mind by paying only for 10 years, rest of the years policy will take care of itself without compromising on benefits

3. Negligible fear of policy lapse

Benefits can be many more. Benefits are customised as per the customer need. Customer is not interested in features or advantages but benefits. Answer WIIFM (What's In It For Me) of the prospect and get a yes faster for policy closure from your prospect.

Power Phrase: If you can't afford Life Insurance now when you have an income, what will happen later? Can you afford not to have Life Insurance?

CHAPTER FOUR

SAVING FORMULA

This technique can be used for existing clients or prospect through online / offline both modes. It is a good conversation starter tool however it can also be used during objection handling time.

Ask - "As per you, what is the formula of saving?"

Most of the people will say that Income minus expenses is equal to savings.

Like this: **Income - Expenses = Savings**

Ask further - how effective is this formula for you?

Listen to answers with full attention. Don't debate. Prospect may say, I don't know the formula.

Say - I learnt another formula of saving from financial experts which is very effective and this formula is income minus saving is equal to expenses.

Recommended formula: Income - Savings = Expenses

Write both formulas in front of prospects. Explain that most of the people try saving through first formula and they miss saving for their goals as there is hardly any money left after meeting expenses.

Effective formula is that you earmarked your savings in advance from your income in the beginning itself whether in a separate bank account or through monthly payment mode. Now you have more control on your money and you don't spend the entire money.

Few prospects may answer this formula. Appreciate these prospects and say that they are making your job easy.

Tell prospect that definition of saving is the sacrifice of small-small happiness of today for a bigger happiness of tomorrow so whatsoever you are doing today for your financial goals will help you in future without doing much worry irrespective of you are there or not.

You can also add that financial experts suggest that one should save minimum 20%-30% of monthly income, are you doing it from the moment you started earning your first income, if not let's take this step today.

Power Phrase: You can borrow money to pay a premium - but you can't borrow health to pass an insurance examination.

CHAPTER FIVE

FREE SERVICE CAMPAIGN

Tell your prospects clearly in the beginning that you are running a free service campaign for all your known people to help them to arrange all their existing policies bought from any of the companies.

If you get any objection; **tell them clearly that you are not going to sell any new policy** to them in this meet and all the details of existing policies will be kept confidential. Tell them that purpose of doing this campaign is to spread awareness amongst people about the benefits of life insurance especially who already bought it.

Request your prospect to share the details through online / offline mode and put the details in excel format or on a piece of paper. You can create a simple format for the same.

Once you enter details of all existing policies in a word / excel sheet etc. then take a print out of the same and post it to your prospect home or convert your word / excel file into a pdf file and mail it. Do remember to add your name, contact no and your profession.

It may happen that you come to know that few policies already matured, lapsed, are in surrender / paid up mode etc. Tell the impact of it to prospect and help him / her for revival / maturity claim etc.

By this way, you will also come to know about the gaps in the financial planning like lack of sufficient insurance cover etc. You may seek a second appointment to discuss about it.

Remember - You need to win the trust of your prospects. There is no hurry that you sell policy in a first meet.

Power Phrase: Some people save to create an estate. Life Insurance Creates an Estate immediately and helps Save.

CHAPTER SIX

HUMAN LIFE VALUE

Ask - "Have you heard about HLV – Human Life Value?" Most of the prospect will say no or would not be able to share the right answer.

Say – HLV is the present value of all future income one will earn till normal retirement age.

Thumb rule of HLV is that everybody should have life insurance cover of minimum 10 times of annual income. E.g. If a customer age is 50 years and his / her annual income is Rs 10 lakh then his / her life insurance cover needs to be minimum Rs 1 Cr. Younger people require a bigger multiple.

Many companies define their HLV grid and they share it with their sellers. You can take the same from your company and show it to your prospects. Maximum Risk Cover allowed is Multiple of Annual Income. Example of one such HLV grid is as follows:

Age Group ....**Maximum Risk Cover allowed**
18-35 ....26-35 Times
36-45 ....16-25 Times
46-50 ....11-15 Times
51-55 ....6-10 Times
56 and above .... up to 5 Times or case to case basis

You can also use the following formula to calculate the net insurance cover of the prospect; you just need to ask **4 simple questions.** Surprisingly, there is no need to ask about income of the prospect at this level:

Q1: What is your net monthly household expenses that needs to be protected (excluding EMIs) e.g. Prospect says Rs 50,000

Add saying that it means Yearly monthly household expenses that needs to be protected for your family: Rs 6,00,000 / year (Rs 50,000 * 12)

Q2: What is the long term fixed deposit rate which you expect on your corpus? E.g. prospect says - 6%

Say to prospect that purpose of asking this question is that normally family prefers to invest this lump sum money of insurance cover in any safe instrument like FD (Fixed Deposit) in case death happens of life assured. So, if we take 6% interest rate then family require a corpus of Rs 1 Crore (6,00,000 / 6%). Divide the annual amount by rate of interest.

Q3: What is your total outstanding principal amount for all types of loan taken as on today? E.g. prospect says Rs 20,00,000

Say to prospect that you are asking this question as financial institutions will demand this amount in lump sum from family if the person dies before paying the entire loan EMIs. So, you need to add this cover in your insurance cover of 1 Cr so total cover required becomes Rs 1.2 Crore.

Q4: How much life insurance you currently have from all life insurance policies? E.g. Rs 40,00,000

Appreciate the prospect that s/he has taken some life insurance cover and say that net life insurance cover required is Rs 80,00,000 (Rs 1,20,00,000 – Rs 40,00,000).

Showing the gap is a big victory. Now it's upto the paying capacity of the customer whether s/he decides to complete the gap in one go or decides to start with a smaller sum assured.

Power Phrase: You plan your foreign trip well in advance and don't leave it to chance. What about your retirement which is sure shot?

CHAPTER SEVEN

OUTSTATION TRIP

Ask - do you go out of your home? If you have to go out of your home for one day only, how much money would you like to handover to your family members so that they can manage expenses for that particular day?

Listen answers without any debate.

Ask - What if you need to go for a week time? Listen answer.

Ask - What if you need to go for a month time? Listen answer.

Ask - Have you ever thought if you might go permanently and that also on happening of unplanned event i.e., death?

Say - I help people to plan for such unplanned events.

Power Phrase: Investments are when money makes money. Life Insurance creates money where none existed before.

CHAPTER EIGHT

DEFINITION OF LIFE INSURANCE

Say - I am doing a survey on life insurance.

Ask - Do you know the definition of life insurance?

Listen and wait for prospect to complete his / her views.

Say - As per life insurance experts, Life insurance is a compensation of financial loss on the happening of an uncertain event like timing of death.

Say - I assist people to minimise the financial loss for the family by proper life insurance planning.

Power Phrase: You can't change what you did in the past, but you can update it. Let's act now.

CHAPTER NINE

NOMINEE

Ask - have you made anyone nominee for your bank accounts, mutual funds or any other investments?

Ask - As per you, what is the purpose of the making nominee?

Say - you must be agreeing to it that the timing of the death is uncertain that's why we make nominee.

Ask - have you reviewed your requirement of life insurance? Is it enough?

Say - As per my experience, more than 90% of my customers were underinsured till they met me.

Ask - Would you like to check the adequacy of life insurance for your goals? I do it free of cost.

Understand the concept of HLV (Human Life Value) given in this book and use it. See the bigger ticket size policies getting closed faster.

Power Phrase: People don't die at the right time. What makes you think it will be different for you?

CHAPTER TEN

Umbrella / Raincoat / Sunglasses / Sunscreen cream

Observe and pick up any one point which is most relatable with your prospect.

Ask - Do you use an umbrella / raincoat / sunglasses / sunscreen cream?

Ask - What's the purpose of keeping / using it?

Listen and wait for prospect to complete his / her views. If required, add few points from your side on the benefits of the same.

Say - Life insurance protects a person during rainy days of life (death, disability, disease) in the similar way umbrella / raincoat protects us from the rain or sunglass / sunscreen cream from the direct sunlight.

Power Phrase: The only difference between an old man and an elderly gentleman is his income.

CHAPTER ELEVEN

FINANCIAL HEALTH CHECK-UP

Ask - when did you go for the health check-up for yourself / family last time? What was the purpose behind it?

Listen without any debate with the prospect.

Say - The way you go for your health check-up to know the status of your health; same way, I do financial health check which helps people like you to know the status of their financial health. This is free of cost for all my existing clients and some special prospects like you.

Complete the basic need analysis and propose your solution.

Power Phrase: Your old age security rests on what you do while young -not on what you think you will do about it a little later.

CHAPTER TWELVE

Vaccination / Mask / Face Shield / PPE Kit

Ask - Have you taken covid vaccination / any of the vaccination for self or any of the family members?

Ask - What's the purpose of this vaccination?

Listen and wait for prospect to complete his / her views. If required, add few points from your side on the benefits of the same.

Say - it prevents / minimise the loss on the person etc. That's the reason that new born kids get vaccination doses from time to time. Life insurance plays the same role in life like vaccination do it for our health.

Alternatively, you can use Mask / Face Shield / PPE (Personal Protective Equipment) kit in the similar way. Pick up the most relatable to your prospect at that time. If customer is wearing a mask, then pick up the topic of mask.

Power Phrase: Leave your wife something that will take care of her, instead of something she will have to take care of.

CHAPTER THIRTEEN

ACCELERATOR AND BREAK

Ask - why do we have brake and accelerator in most of our 2/4 wheelers even if there is no clutch pedal?

Listen and wait for prospect to complete his / her views. If required, add few points from your side on the benefits of the same.

Say - Speed thrills and helps us to reach our destination faster while brake helps us to control the speed of our vehicle. Life insurance is like a brake to the vehicle. It provides guarantee to the life so that one can take risk in the form of speed, to put rest of the money in equity, real estate etc. and earn high interest.

Say - Both are equally important, speed without break is of no use and break without speed is not required.

Power Phrase: Life Insurance is like fun - the older you get, the more it costs - and the harder it is to get.

CHAPTER FOURTEEN

FUNERAL

Say - please allow me to ask one uncomfortable question. Have you ever gone to funerals so far?

Wait for the response. Listen carefully and give verbal and non-verbal signals like nodding, saying hmm....etc.

Ask – How many of these deaths were untimely deaths?

Say – most of the deaths are untimely deaths and these people never planned for these deaths. They were like you and me and left their families.

Given a choice, would you like to leave your family happy or crying on daily basis for basic needs of the life.

Say - I assist people to plan in such a way that no body dies without proper financial planning.

Power Phrase: Life Insurance is time... time you might not have to complete the goals you've planned. If you need time, you need Life Insurance. Do you need time?

Health / Motor / Property / Fire Insurance

Ask - Do you have any insurance like health / motor / property / fire etc.?

Ask - What's the purpose of buying these insurance covers?

Listen and wait for prospect to complete his / her views. If required, add few points from your side on the benefits of the same.

Say - The way these items cover medical / other expenses for you / your family, life insurance covers your dreams in the similar way towards your family or covers your income earning capacity in case of death, disability, critical illness etc.

Power Phrase: Unless you have a rich uncle, the only money you will have at retirement age is the money you don't spend now.

CHAPTER SIXTEEN

DATE OF DEATH

Say - Can I ask you one comfortable question? You must be knowing your date of birth but do you also know your date of death?

Listen and wait for prospect to complete his / her views.

Say - In fact, none of us know our date of death. Early death and late death both are risks. In early death, risk is born by the family members while risk of the late death is born by the person himself / herself. I assist people to protect both types of risk.

Ask - On which one, you would like to start planning – Early death or late death?

Power Phrase: Would you agree that the only person who can take care of the older person you will someday be - is the younger person you are now?

CHAPTER SEVENTEEN

MAGICAL QUESTIONS

Say - I am going to ask few questions for analysing your need for long term financial goals. I would like to make notes of your answer so that I can propose a suitable solution for the same. I hope same is ok with you?

Ask the following questions one by one, listen to the answers given by the prospect and keep noting the answers.

- What is your top long term financial goal which is not planned fully?
- Why is this your top priority?
- How would you feel if you have done all financial arrangements and achieve this goal?
- How would you feel if that event comes but you don't have sufficient money required for this goal?
- How much money you require for it in present value?
- How much is already arranged?
- What is the inflation rate to be taken to calculate the future value of this goal?
- How much money you can invest monthly to meet the gap?

You need to demonstrate a great level of verbal and non-verbal communication. Use voice modulation appropriately.

Remember - Asking questions is an art and it can be learned. You need to practice it.

Power Phrase: Most men buy life insurance because they once fell in love with a girl and decided to support her as long as she might live.

CHAPTER EIGHTEEN

HELMET / SEAT BELT / AIR BAGS / LIFE JACKET

Observe and speak.

If customer is using a 2-wheeler, **ask**, "Do you have helmet for your 2-wheeler?" What's the purpose of helmet?

If customer is using a 4-wheeler, **ask**, "Do you use seat belt in your car or how many air bags are in your car?" What is the purpose of a seat belt / air bag in a car?"

If customer is a frequent flyer, **ask**, "Why flights have life jackets under every seat?" Would you like to take one such flight in which you don't have a life jacket under your seat?

Listen and wait for prospect to complete his / her views. If required, add few points from your side on the benefits of the same.

Say - Life insurance protects income earning capacity in the similar way helmet / seat belt / air bag / life jacket protects us or minimise the losses from accident.

Power Phrase: The heaviest burden for a man to carry in the late afternoon (Retirement) of his life is an empty purse.

GIFT

Say - In your life, you must have received and given many **GIFTs** to your family members like to your spouse, children, grandchildren, parents etc? What if I tell you that you can give them the **most memorable GIFT?**

Say - Let me share how it works.

Your near one will get a guaranteed regular income on every birthday / marriage anniversary 10 years from now for 20/25/30 years regularly.

By doing this, they remember you throughout their life and you show love and affection towards them.

Would you like to know more about it? Explain your product in detail which matches above benefits. Show cost in the last.

Power Phrase: Do you know anyone with a lease on life? It's not a question of if...it's a question of when.

CHAPTER TWENTY

FIRE EXTINGUISHER / SPRINKLER

Ask - Do you have any Fire Extinguisher / Sprinkler in your office / home / society / factory? Listen to the answer.

Ask - What's the purpose of installing these equipments?

Listen and wait for prospect to complete his / her views. If required, add few points from your side on the benefits of the same.

Say - The way Fire Extinguisher / Sprinkler helps you to protect the property and people in case of fire, in the similar way life insurance covers your dreams and income earning capacity in case of any mishappening.

Power Phrase: There is never a convenient time to start saving money. Like turning on a cold shower - never pleasant, never convenient, it feels wonderful after you do it.

CHAPTER TWENTY-ONE

DAHINA HAATH (THE RIGHT HAND)

Say - "Have you heard about the words, "You are my dahina haath (the right hand)?"

If yes, what is the meaning of these words?

Listen with full attention. If customer answers it correctly, appreciate the answer. If customer is not able to answer it or answers it partially, say, **the right-hand means**:

- An extremely efficient or reliable person
- A person who stands with you at all time especially in case of urgency
- A person who is your back up in case you fall ill or not available"

Say:

- Do you have such persons in your personal life who are real right hands?
- Congrats (If customer says yes) for having right hand persons in your life
- Today, I am here to discuss one (more) such person who can be a real right hand for you and your family
- Purpose is that you and your family should not suffer like many other people suffer when they don't have any right-hand person

in their life
- Would you like to know more about this person?

If customer says yes, choose the most suitable product and write it's benefits on a piece of paper. Say that this product is playing the role of the right hand for many of your existing customers.

Once you write all benefits; say, to get these benefits, you just need to pay a small cost and mention the premium amount.

Power Phrase: Someone always pays a life insurance premium; the head of the family while s/he is alive; or his/her dependents who live on after him/her.

CHAPTER TWENTY-TWO

RENTED HOME VERSUS OWN HOME

Dear Customer, may I **ask** whether this home is on rent or it's your own? Ask this question if you are unsure about the ownership of house else no need to ask this question.

If customer says – It's my own home then move to the next question.

Ask – What are the benefits of buying own home instead of a rented home?

Drive to the points like proud feeling, freedom, comfort, social status, necessity, peace of mind etc.

Say – Life Insurance is like this home which gives you more freedom, proud feeling, comfort, social status, necessity, peace of mind etc. It is not optional but a necessity now a days.

Power Phrase: Compare the cost of having it and not needing it with the cost of needing it and not having it.

CHAPTER TWENTY-THREE

IMPACT OF INFLATION

Ask your prospect, **"Do you know the impact of inflation on your long-term financial goals like child education, child marriage, creating a corpus for your dream home / office / retirement?"**

If customer says, "Yes, I know." Congratulate him / her.

Ask - "Would you like to reconfirm it with me?" If yes, ask for the goal, tenure, amount required in today's value and expected inflation rate. If customer does not know the impact of inflation, ask the same questions from him / her.

Use any inflation calculator online by entering above details and show the future value of the goal to the prospect considering the impact of the inflation.

Future Value of Goal: Current Value of the goal * Inflation factor (to be picked in front of the term chosen by customer)

Example: Customer A wants Rs 10,00,000 in today's value for his / her son / daughter's education after 20 years at 5% inflation. What will be the future value of Goal?

Answer: Future Value of Goal: Rs 10,00,000 * 2.6533 = Rs 26,53,300

Assumptions: Inflation factor taken @ 5% and up to 4 decimals.

Ask - how much saving / corpus has been already planned for this goal. Congratulate customer for the same and reduce the corpus amount from this future value. If customer has not planned anything for this goal; say, "Don't worry, it's not too late. I am here to assist you to plan for the same."

Example: Customer has done some saving in the above example and s/he will get Rs 6,53,300 after 20 years so the final gap for the goal is Rs 20,00,000 (Rs 26,53,300 - Rs 6,53,300)

Ask - do you want to meet this gap even if you are there or you are not there? If yes, I have a guaranteed way to achieve this goal. Pitch your life insurance product which gives the gap amount as maturity amount in lump sum. Highlight that the goal is protected from day one because of the insurance cover.

Power Phrase: The only person who gambles on life insurance is the person who goes without it. This person doesn't carry the risk – his/her family does.

CHAPTER TWENTY-FOUR

ADOPTED CHILD

Say it to prospect, "Today I am going to ask few questions from you and expecting an honest reply on the same. **First question** is that to raise a child from birth till making him / her independent, how much money you spend on an average / year on him / her?"

You will get different answers from all prospects depending upon their economical background. Let's take an example, prospect says Rs 2 lakh / year on an average for first 20 years and total Rs 40 lakhs.

Say it to prospect, "Thanks, being a parent we all spend money on our kids for their better future. I pray to God that your child really excels in life and do well in future however let me **ask you an uncomfortable question** – Whether you will feel comfortable to ask money from your child once you retire from your regular work and now your child is financially independent."

Listen to prospect and don't miss the eye contact. Say, **today I am going to share a wonderful concept of "Adopted Child"**. Draw a time line (a straight horizontal line) and explain it step by step to your prospect. Alternatively, you can keep a readymade time line graph with standard example of Rs 1 lakh, Rs 2 lakh and Rs 5 lakh premiums etc.

Say to prospect, "Treat this as another child of yours where you need to invest to raise this child only for next 10/12 years with the same amount as you are doing on your child e.g. Rs 2 lakh / annum. So, you invested total Rs 20/24 Lakh on this child in 10/12 years.

Now just wait for 1/2/3/5 years and this adopted child starts giving you guaranteed returns for next 25/30/35 years or till life time. This per year amount will be approximately the same amount or higher amount which you invested on this child per year.

Additionally this child will also give you / your nominee guaranteed lump sum corpus at the end of term or at the time of death. This corpus will be approximately the entire amount which you paid to raise this child e.g. in this case, around 20 / 24 lakh etc.

Customize this pitch, term, guaranteed return amount etc as per your company product. Preferably, pitch it for guaranteed products of your company although this pitch can be used for any saving plan.

Power Phrase: If every wife knew what every widow knows, every husband would carry more Life Insurance.

CHAPTER TWENTY-FIVE

MOBILE TEMPERED GLASS / MOBILE COVER

Ask - Do you use mobile tempered glass / mobile cover for your mobile?

Ask - What's the purpose of mobile tempered glass / mobile cover?

Listen and wait for prospect to complete his / her views. If required, add few points from your side on the benefits of the same.

Say - Life insurance protects income earning capacity in the similar way mobile tempered glass / mobile cover protects the mobile or it minimizes the losses from accidents.

Power Phrase: Will Rogers once said, "If a man doesn't believe in Life Insurance, let him die once without any. That will teach him a lesson."

CHAPTER TWENTY-SIX

PRODUCT CLOSURE

Use this pitch when a good life insurance product is getting closed or returns are getting decreased or premiums rates are increasing shortly.

This pitch works on the simple philosophy that **people either buy due to fear of loss or chance of gain**.

Approach your prospects **saying** that you are contacting all your prospects / existing customers to share this valuable information that one of the most sellable / good products of your company which is very beneficial for customers like you, is reducing returns due to current market scenario. Last date to buy this product is.....

Keeping above in mind, I want to meet you for 15-20 minutes to explain its benefits to you.

Power Phrase: You have only given to your kids throughout your life so why to expect money from them when you retire.

Stories

"The Universe is made of stories and not of atoms." By – Muriel Rukeyser

We all love stories from our childhood. Stories are one of the best ways to engage people. You get undivided attention of your prospects.

Storytelling is an art. You need to work on your voice modulation, body language before you start narrating stories to others.

When basic rapport is built with prospect or you already know your prospect then you can start sharing stories with your prospect in an informal way. You need to select such stories which can be linked with **the importance of life insurance, Standard of Living, Rapport building, Product pitching, Conversation Starter, Legacy planning, Child Education, Wealth Creation, Pricing, Objection handling or closing etc.**

These stories can emerge anytime whether in the beginning, middle, last part of conversation especially when prospect procrastinate the decison to buy life insurance again and again.

Let me tell you that you will find out right time for the same. Just trust your instinct.

Right practice will make you a great story teller.

Remember, great sales people are great story tellers.

CHAPTER TWENTY-SEVEN

5 THIRSTY BROTHERS AND A LAKE

There were 5 brothers who were roaming in a jungle. They were very thirsty and were searching for water. They all moved into different directions to search for the water. The youngest one found it out first.

He never saw such a big and beautiful lake in his life. It was mesmerizing to see such a clean water. For few seconds he forgot about his thurst. Then he bent towards water to drink it but before he could touch the water one image came out of the lake and said: I am the owner of this lake; if you want to drink water of this lake then you need to answer my questions else this water will become poisonous and you will die immediately.

This youngest brother ignored this warning and drank the water. As warned by owner of the lake, he died immediately. Same fate happened with his 3 elder brothers one by one when they came searching for water and other brothers.

Now the eldest brother came and he saw that all his 4 younger brothers were dead. He was totally shocked however his thrust was such that he also bent towards water to drink it. Same image came out of water and warned him that he can also die like his younger brothers if he tried to drink water without answering his questions.

This elder brother thought that it's better to attempt answering his questions so he said to owner of the lake that go ahead and ask your questions. This owner asked many questions and this elder brother answered it one by one. He asked one very interesting question from this elder brother, **"What is the ultimate truth of life which everyone knows but no one is ready to accept it."**

Ask - would you like to guess the answer given by this eldest brother. Be totally silent after asking this question. Don't disturb prospect thoughts. Most of the prospect knows answer and will answer you correctly.

In case prospect is not able to answer it; tell prospect that s/he can take time for next 1-2 days and answer it. If prospect insist you to answer then **say** that this elder brother said **"DEATH"** as answer of this question. Owner of the lake was very happy to get all right answers and all his brothers who were dead became alive. He allowed all of them to drink water as well.

Say - this story is applicable to each one of us. We may want to ignore this topic but it's the ultimate and bitter truth of life. You may postpone your decision to buy your life insurance policy for next week, month or year due to any of the reasons which may sound very genuine at this point of time to you but are you 100% sure that you will be there to buy it later?

So why not to decide today and have a complete peace of mind for self and family.

Power Phrase: It's far easier to pay for college over 12 or 15 years, than 4 years.

CHAPTER TWENTY-EIGHT

SISYPHUS

Ask - Have you heard the story of the King Sisyphus? If not, let me share few details about him.

Say - As per Wikipedia - In Greek mythology Sisyphus or Sisyphos was the founder and king of Ephyra. He was punished for cheating death twice by being forced to roll an immense boulder up a hill only for it to roll down every time it neared the top, repeating this action for eternity.

Say - This story is very similar with humans. Treat this boulder as standard of living and one continuously pushes himself / herself to move upwards but there are few uncertainties of life like untimely death, disability, critical illness, accidents etc. which pushes it downwards.

What if you have **"WEDGE"** (a piece of metal, wood, rubber etc. with a pointed edge at one end and a wide edge at the other side - See the picture in the next page) so that you can put it under the boulder henceforth this boulder does not go down further.

Now relate all type of **insurances as "Wedge"** for you. While you are continuously pushing yourself to improve your standard of living upwards but **what if any unplanned event comes e.g. death, disability, accidents.** What will happen to your standard of living if no insurance is in place?

Protect your standard of living and other assets with right type of insurance, today.

You can share this story through social media or one to one with your prospects. Then relate that you sell "Wedge" in the form of insurance.

Do remember, people love to listen to stories or concepts. Make it interesting.

Power Phrase: No person plans to be poor when s/he reaches his / her mid-sixties, the trouble lies in not planning to be.

Wedge

CHAPTER TWENTY-NINE

MONEY MINTING MACHINE

Say - Few months back, I went to one of the Goa beaches in the early morning. I was alone, enjoying morning breeze and sea waves. The Sun was rising behind the sea.

Suddenly, I saw a bottle with a cork on it. I observed that this bottle was moving. It increased my curiosity. Hesitantly; I removed the cork from the bottle.

To my surprise, initially some smoke came out of it and then I saw the biggest surprise of my life. Here comes a very nice; Blue colour Jinn out of it, saying **"Kya Hukam hai mere aaka means what are your commands for me?"**

I asked him whether you can provide a **"Money Minting Machine"** to me as that will fulfil most of my wishes.

Jinn smiled and said; Yes, I can but there will be **3 terms and conditions** before I provide the same to you. These are:

1. You can print only Rs 10 lakh / year
2. This machine is not replaceable
3. You can get this machine only once

I told the Jinn that it's acceptable to me thinking that I will take insurance on this machine. Suddenly, I saw my daughter trying to wake me up. Oh...this was a dream. On the other side, I was relating it to our life.

Say - We as **human beings are money minting machines** as we earn some money every year, this human life is not replaceable and we get it only once.

We are also privileged to protect our income (Money Minting Machine) through life insurance if it's sufficient. Life insurance cover will depend on your age, yearly income, policy term, health status etc.

Ask - **Have you secured your "Money Minting Machine"?** If not, what stopped you to do this? I can assist you to secure your money Minting machine. Would you like to know more about it? Explain once you get go ahead from the customer.

Power Phrase: Paying premium isn't the problem. Paying the premium is the solution.

CHAPTER THIRTY

TICKET FOR THE SHIP

Say - Few days back, I went to a customer home. Customer was sitting along with his wife and 5 years old daughter.

During introduction, his daughter asked her father that what this uncle (means I) do. Her father asked me to explain my role to his daughter.

I said to his daughter by addressing her name, just imagine that your father has to go outside country for his office work via sea. If he takes a small boat then it will be very risky as there are lots of shark in the sea water. Another option is that your father goes through a very big ship along with many people like him. Since this ship is very big, sharks can't attack and it's totally safe to travel. **My role is to sell tickets for this big ship so that your papa is totally safe, your mom and you should not get worry for your papa.**

Daughter immediately asked her father to buy the ticket for the big ship and father said – ok.

Say – Small boat indicates the journey of a person without any life insurance, shark indicates death, disability, disease, accident etc. Risk is higher in a small boat while big ship indicates the safety of travelling with other people who has taken similar risk. They have pooled money in such a way that remaining people can take care of the family of the deceased etc.

Say - "This story is applicable to each one of us who is a bread winner for the family." Henceforth, I assist people like you who are responsible heads of their families.

Power Phrase: Your widow's most cherished memories of your good intentions will not pay the rent or the grocer's bill.

CHAPTER THIRTY-ONE

BAGHBAN

Please see "Baghban" a Bollywood movie before you narrate this story to your prospects. This story is on the need of retirement planning.

Ask - "Have you seen Baghban movie?" If yes, can I request you to share the story of this movie briefly. Appreciate prospect if s/he tells it else say - In this movie, Amitabh and Hema are playing the role of husband, wife. They were having 4 sons. They also helped one orphan boy (played by Salman Khan) to complete his studies by paying his fees and other expenses.

All 4 sons got good education, good jobs, got married and had kids. It was decided that Amitabh and Hema will stay with them separately for 3 months each. Both parents had big issues staying with their sons and family. They were not able to meet each other.

Amitabh wrote a book on the struggle of his life named as "Baghban." The orphan boy helped them to reunite, stay with dignity and publication of this book. Book was sold like a hot cake. Amitabh earned a lot of money from this book.

They left their 4 sons and started staying alone. The message from this movie was – Can you depend on your family especially during retirement phase?

Say, "It will be an ideal scenario if you have caring son / daughter who might take care of you in your retirement time however why to keep yourself dependant on your kids while you can plan for your retirement right now."

Power Phrase: If you have no dependent, have you someone on whom you can depend in old age for support? Do you know, "The misery of a baby is interesting to its mother, the misery of a young man is interesting to a young woman, the misery of an old man is interesting to nobody.

CHAPTER THIRTY-TWO

REAL LIFE STORY

Say - this incident is from a nearby town where Veer lived with his wife and daughter.

Tell them that your manager and you went to meet Veer at his home.

Veer was convinced about the product and was ready to buy the life insurance plan.

In the last moment, his wife denied to buy it immediately and said that we will buy it later on.

Next month, they all went to a hill station to enjoy summer holidays.

While coming back, Veer was in a separate car, car break failed and his car met with an accident. He died on spot. In-laws asked wife and daughter to move out of their home as they were not having enough funds.

Wife and daughter started staying at a rented place with a lot of worries about school fees, routine expenses etc.

We came to know about this accident. We went to meet his wife and daughter and asked them to search the documents of Veer's life insurance policy.

Wife started crying that it's my fault that I only denied it so there is no such policy.

We said – Mam, Veer sir called us in his office on the same day and bought a policy of Rs 50 lakh Sum assured so find out the policy.

They found the policy, claim settled within 1 week and they got Rs 50 lakhs.

Wife and daughter restarted the life and this amount helped them to maintain the standard of living.

Due to this incident, I took an oath to spread the awareness about life insurance so that it does not happen with anybody else.

Given a choice, **would you like to leave your family on fate or protect all your goals towards your family?**

Note: This story is given as a back-up story. You shall pick up any real-life story from your city ideally known to you else you can modify the same story by replacing names with local names.

Power Phrase: Life Insurance is designed to relieve economic pressure, and when applied by an expert, always works.

CHAPTER THIRTY-THREE

THE GRANDPARENTS

Say – My Client's family consist of Husband, wife and 2 kids named as Priyanka and Priyank.

Both kids get surprise birthday gift every year but these gifts are not from parents but their grandparents.

They remember their grandparents who planned such gifts for them. Both kids remember their grandparents very fondly with their full names. Other kids in the similar age group don't remember their grandparents.

Grandparents took such life insurance policies where grandchildren will get regular guaranteed money every year for next 30-40 years on their birthdays. They were proposer / payee while the grand children were life insured.

If you also want that your grandchildren shall remember you in the similar way? If yes, I have a solution. Explain your product accordingly. Ideally your product should offer guaranteed income or whole life income options.

Note: This story should be narrated ideally to grandparents and with parents in some cases.

Power Phrase: One of two things is certain; you will live or die. If you live, you will need money; if you die, your family will.

CHAPTER THIRTY-FOUR

BUSINESS CONTINUITY

Say – Let me tell you about one of my clients Mr. Aiyar. He is a big business person.

Client's family consist of Husband, wife and 2 sons – Venu and Pravin.

Venu was interested for job while Pravin was interested for the family business.

Father was worried for equal asset division amongst both sons.

Father took Endowment plan in such a way that Venu can get money equal to the value of the business.

Father survived. His dream of continuation of business fulfilled. Policy maturity amount was given to Venu. All of them are at peace of mind, business continued without any fight or division of business.

As mentioned in this real-life incident, would you like to plan for your family in such a way that there is no need to withdraw money at once from the business and it does not impact business negatively?

Wait for the customer response. Explain endowment / ULIP product where customer can get lumpsum amount. Link it with the son / daughter's name.

Note: This story is for example purpose. You can use this by saying that this is a real story of a client served by your branch /

company. Pick up any other story with local characters. Focus on the business continuity.

Power Phrase: Show me a person who owns adequate life insurance and knows why s/he owns it, and I'll show you a person who's happy.

CHAPTER THIRTY-FIVE

2 RAASTE (WAYS)

Say – Once upon a time, there were 2 friends who were working together for many years.

They found details of a treasure.

When they checked, they found that they require one more person for this task as only two of them were not sufficient.

They called many people for interviews and finally shortlisted two out of them for the final round of selection.

They told them that they will conduct a final test and whosoever clears the test will be selected for this work.

They took both candidates on a cross road and told them that both ways look exactly same but one way will lead to the right destination while other one will not lead to it.

Saying this, both friends moved on.

Out of two selected candidates, one candidate decided to go on the left way while second candidate stood on the same thinking which way will be the right one.

After few hours, 1st candidate was coming back so 2nd candidate thought that this was the wrong way henceforth 2nd way is the right way.

Before he could decide to walk on the 2nd way, 1st candidate moved from the 1st way to the 2nd way.

Suddenly, both friends came out of the bushes. They were hiding there itself.

They said – Both of you, come back immediately. We have shortlisted one candidate, it's candidate no 1 who chose to go on the wrong path and they rejected 2nd candidate by saying that you were just thinking while first one acted.

Ask - What's the learning from this story? Listen to the views without any debate.

Say - Same way – people who decide faster gets success even if they go on the wrong way. It's your turn, treasure is waiting in the form of life insurance on the other side, only, if you take the first step.

Note: You can use this story especially with those prospects who procrastinate to take a decision on buying life insurance.

Power Phrase: The risk exists; it's just a question of who holds the bag- your spouse and kiddies, or the Life Insurance Company.

CHAPTER THIRTY-SIX

PEBLO AND BRUNO – BUCKET VS PIPELINE

Say - Once upon a time, in a village, there was scarcity of water.

Peblo and Bruno 2 friends were carrying buckets filled with water, from a nearby river and supplying it to villagers. By doing this, they were earning some money and were just surviving.

Peblo was unhappy with this income and he started working to arrange a pipeline from river towards the village while Bruno continued the same practice with a larger water bucket.

Peblo took some time but did it and became super rich while Bruno stuck at the same level.

Ask - What's the learning from this story? Listen to the views without any debate.

Say - Same is with taking decision at the right time to buy a right life insurance policy. It takes some time but you get a pipeline of income. Would you like to understand about one such solution which provides a steady flow of big income? Let me explain it to you. Explain the product.

Power Phrase: You are your family's trustee. The question is - are you a good trustee?

CHAPTER THIRTY-SEVEN

IF BUFFALO DIES

Say - Once upon a time; in a small village; there were 2 friends, Sonu and Monu. One day they saw a luxury car. Sonu said to Monu, I want to buy this car after 3 years. I have a business idea. Would you like to know about it? Monu said yes.

Sonu said; we will buy a buffalo; sell the milk; will re-invest the money; buy another buffalo; sell more milk; buy more buffalos then we will open a dairy, will sell more milk, butter, ghee, paneer etc. By doing this, we will earn a lot of money in 3 years and will be able to buy the luxury car. Monu agreed with this idea and both departed by saying that we will meet after 3 years with our luxury cars.

Sonu came back to the village exactly after 3 years in a luxury car in a nice suit and stopped his car in front of Monu's house. Monu was sitting outside his house. He was not able to recognize Sonu. Sonu said, "Don't you remember me; I am your friend Sonu, we decided to start a business 3 years ago. I followed exactly the way; we planned and became one of the richest persons in the city in 3 years. So, I bought this dream luxury car. Where is your car?"

Monu said, "Sorry, I don't have car. 3 years back, when our meeting was over, I went back to my home and I discussed the business idea with my wife. My wife said, "What if first buffalo dies?" I was not having any answer to this question. So, I did not start this business and not earned any extra money to buy a luxury car.

Ask - What is your learning from this story? Listen with full attention without any debate with prospect.

Say – Many customers postpone their buying decisions for life insurance due to various ifs but they forget the real IFs of life i.e. what if death, disability, accident, critical illness happens. I assist people to answer these ifs. **Lets decide today itself to answer few of these ifs of life.**

Power Phrase: Life Insurance enables a man to accomplish - immediately - what otherwise would be the work of a lifetime.

CHAPTER THIRTY-EIGHT

THE BARASINGHA (SWAMP DEER)

Once upon a time, there was a big jungle and there lived a Barasingha.

He used to be sad by looking at his feet as it looked ugly while his horns were looking so good.

One day, a hunter came, Barasingha was caught in a net due to his horns, few friends helped him to cut the net and release him. His dirty feet helped him to run faster and save his life.

Ask - What's the learning from this story? Listen to the views without any debate.

Say - Same is with assets. Treat horns like risky investment and feet as secured investment like life insurance. We require both in our life. Investing only through risky investment can put you in trouble. I assist people like you to keep a balance of both.

Note: Key message is diversification and the role of life insurance for this asset allocation.

Power Phrase: Life Insurance makes your money work for you when you are through working for it.

CHAPTER THIRTY-NINE

THE MANGO ORCHARD

Say - this story is about a farmer Ramu:

- A farmer who started with a mango orchard.
- He took utmost care of this orchard for first 8-10 years
- He started getting good quality and quantity fruits from 10th year onwards for the next 30-40 years
- Even if he dies, his family will get benefits for his efforts

Say - my services are like this mango orchard where you need to put your time and money for first 10 years only.

- After that, it will give regular harvest to you / your family for the next 30-40 years
- Everyone in the family remembers the name of this farmer even after his death
- Pitch a guaranteed income product by explaining benefits first and then sharing the cost per year

Power Phrase: Life Insurance offers a person the only way where she can make her will before she makes her money.

CHAPTER FORTY

STORY OF GURU, DISCIPLE AND HAPPINESS

Say – Once upon a time, there was a Guru and his disciple. Disciple completed his education and requested for permission of his guru to move on from his ashram so that he could share his learnings to the entire world.

Guru thought to check the final readiness of the disciple so accompanied him for some distance. During the journey Disciple asked from the Guru, "What is happiness?" Guru: What is your understanding of happiness so far? Disciple: Happiness is when one has something to eat, a roof to cover head and some work to do.

Guru just smiled but did not say anything. After some distance, they saw a Poultry Farm where lots of hens were roaming around. Guru asked – these hens have something to eat, roof and some work to do (lay eggs), is this happiness? Disciple got confused however said yes as it meets all 3 criteria as told by him.

They further travelled and saw lots of hens in an open area of a very big jungle. It was not a poultry farm. Hens were moving around freely although there was a risk that any big animal could kill / eat them. Guru asked disciple again – Are these hens happy or hens of poultry farm were happier.

Disciple said – Open jungle hens are happier than the poultry farm hens as they have freedom although this freedom comes on the cost of a higher risk. Guru said – that is the answer of your question asked in the beginning on happiness.

Disciple said – Yes, I understood it very well.

Say – this is exactly what we are offering to the people; **we are offering freedom to the people in the form of life insurance**. We recommend sufficient and need based life insurance to people which leads to peace of mind and the ultimate happiness for the insured and family.

Power Phrase: "Play Fair" with your spouse. If conditions were reversed--how much life insurance would you want her to carry?

CHAPTER FORTY-ONE

THE ANTS AND THE GRASSHOPPER

Say – Once upon a time; during summer season, ants were working hard to collect the food and store it for the winter season. Grasshopper laughed at them and said that you are fools. One should only think about the present and should not worry about future. He danced all the day, enjoying and did not collect any food for winter.

After few months, winter started. Grasshopper was dying due to hunger. He requested ants to help him but they denied it as food was just enough for them. Grasshopper died due to hunger.

Ask - What message do you get from this story? Listen with interest.

Say - This is how life insurance works. Whatsoever one contributes today as a premium, it will help the family in future during the time when it's needed most.

Power Phrase: To buy life insurance, you need the willingness to give up something today so that your family would not have to give up everything tomorrow.

CHAPTER FORTY-TWO

REVERSE FORMULA

Let me share one interesting story with you. In a small village, there was a small boy "Kaku" who lived happily with his family.

There was a Mango orchard outside the village. One day, when he was passing it; he saw lots of Mangoes; ready to eat. There were 3 gates back-to-back to enter in the Mango orchard and every gate was guarded by one security guard each. They were kind enough to allow him to enter the Mango orchard but with a SMALL condition.

This small condition was, "You can pluck any number of mangoes but you need to give half of the mangoes at each gate to each guard".

Kaku wanted 3 mangoes while moving out from the orchard after crossing all 3 gates but this condition put him in confusion.

He is now seeking your help to tell him the number of mangoes to be plucked from the orchard. What will be your answer?

If you found the answer, just reflect how you calculated this number. Whether it was a hit and trial method or you found the right formula. What if I say that Kaku wanted 19 mangoes instead of 3 and you have just 10 seconds to answer?

First thing first, if Kaku wanted 3 mangoes then he needs to have double of it i.e., 6 mangoes at the last exit gate, double of this number at middle gate i.e., 12 mangoes and double of it at the 3rd gate i.e., 24 mangoes. So; you double the end / required number 3 times, this formula is called the "Reverse Formula".

It's applicable everywhere in life. If you want to go to the airport from your home, you do the reverse calculation and accordingly you leave your home to catch the flight.

You require 1 Crore after 20 years for your retirement or other goals; have you done the reverse calculation to know the exact amount to be saved per year to reach the goal?

I assist people to do such work especially when these goals are important and critical ones for self and family.

Power Phrase: It doesn't make much difference to a widow whether her husband's Life Insurance was bought with premium or discounted Rupees - provided he left her some Life Insurance.

CHAPTER FORTY-THREE

KALPVRIKSH (A TREE WHO FULFIL ALL WISHES)

Say - A person was doing Tapasya (Austerity) of God for a long time.

After a long time, God appeared and asked him / her about his / her wish.

S/he said, I want Kalpvriksh who can fulfil all my wishes.

God gifted him a Kalpvriksh with a condition that you need to give water to this tree only once and it will fulfil your wishes for life time / many years.

Say - I help people to have such trees in their homes, would you like to have one such tree in your home? This tree is in the form of life insurance single premium option where you pay it only once like watering once to the kalpvriksh and then it will take care of fruits for many years. Explain the benefits first by using customer name in between and tell premium in last.

Power Phrase: You have frequently heard a young man say, "I have all the life insurance I want" but you have yet to hear an old man say, "I have bought all the life insurance I need for my old age."

Activities

Activities involves both the prospect and the seller. It comes with a pinch of surprise, curiosity, and suspense.

It works on kinaesthetic learning principle - that people learn many things by doing it or experiencing it instead of just listening or reading about life insurance.

Tip: Practice and try these activities with your friends, colleagues before using it with your prospects.

CHAPTER FORTY-FOUR

VISITING CARD WITH A HOLE

Do a single punch / hole with the help of a punching machine on your visiting card anywhere in the empty area where nothing is printed. See the photo in the next page.

When you handover this card to a prospect via online or face to face, prospect's focus will be on this hole as nobody ever did this in the past with him/her.

Chances are high that prospect will ask you about hole, even if prospect does not ask then also you can say **"This hole is similar with my role, my role as a life insurance professional is to find out holes / gaps in the financial planning of people like you and then assisting them with a solution to fill the gap."**

Do remember that you need to keep many such visiting cards in your visiting card holder before you visit prospect place. Do remember that first impressions make your job easy and prospect is more attentive towards you.

Note: Don't punch the card in front of the prospect else there is no fun in it. Don't punch on company logo, name or other details else it will look bad.

Power Phrase: When you die, there are four deaths: the husband, the father, the son and the income. Life Insurance can't bring back rest 3 but it can bring back income if sufficient life insurance is bought.

Visiting Card With a Hole

CHAPTER FORTY-FIVE

MISSION PLANTATION

Call your prospects and share that you have taken a **mission to contribute in the environment henceforth you are distributing free plants to all families known in your circle.** You want to meet and gift this plant to the prospect.

Take appointment, meet the prospect and help the prospect to fix it in a pot.

Once done, say that life insurance is also like this plant which gets started like a small plant but once you give it water, care regularly then it gives you good results in the form of oxygen, flowers, medicines, and fruits. Your company has launched a new product which gives multiple benefits under this product.

Ask - Shall I share some details quickly with you?

Say, "Just understand it, you are not bound to buy it immediately." Do the basic need analysis and explain benefits of your product. Take feedback about it. Connect it again with plant, observe body language and close the deal at an appropriate time.

Power Phrase: What is the best time to buy a life insurance policy? First best time was when you started earning and second-best time is today if you are still insurable.

CHAPTER FORTY-SIX

3 Names who will take care of the family

You need to carry your visiting cards in a nice visiting card holder. It should be printed from one side only and back side need to be totally clean and empty. Just write following on the back side of visiting card in advance before visiting to the prospect

S. No. Name

1.

2.

3.

After your own basic introduction, handover this visiting card from the side where this 1,2,3 is written to prospect and say, **"Mr./Ms Prospect; I am doing a small survey to find out that how many people have 3 names who will take care of their family financially in the same way like they do, in case they die tomorrow."**

I did this survey with hundreds of people but nobody could write even a single name so far. Sir/Mam, can you think of 3 names who will take care of your family financially in the same way like you do in your absence if you die tomorrow."

Entire exercise is on your voice modulation and how are you showing your emotions during this exercise. You can handover a pen to prospect if required and be totally silent. Don't disturb prospect's thoughts.

If prospect asks for clarification, then clarify that it's not the survival of family but focus is on the words **"the same way like you do"** e.g., if currently you change your car every 3 year whether family would be able to do it if you die tomorrow or after 5 years or after 10 years etc.

Most prospects will say no that I never thought about it and I don't have any name. Now turn the card and say, **"I have at least one name and that name is (say your life insurance company name) who will take care of your family financially in the same way like you, if you have sufficient insurance."**

That's the purpose of my meeting with you for today. With your permission, I want to do a proper need analysis and suggest solutions accordingly? Shall I go ahead.

Note: If prospect still writes any name and says that s/he has 1/2/3 names; say congrats to him/her; say that you are extremely happy to know about it as today you found first prospect that have at least 1/2/3 name/s.

Ask - whether it will be a good idea to check with these names whether they know about it or not so that you are doubly sure about it. Let customer call them and tell them that s/he has written their name for this purpose. Enjoy what happens next. Do remember that you are not arguing with prospect but genuinely interested for his/her family well-being.

Power Phrase: One ordinary father can support four children. But it takes four extra-ordinary children to support one father.

CHAPTER FORTY-SEVEN

DICE

Carry a small dice and a chocolate with you.

Say – This is a dice consisting of no 1 to 6, you will get 3 chances for number 6 to show up. If you get 6 then you will get a chocolate. Handover dice to the prospect to throw it randomly.

If customer gets a 6 within first 3 chances – **Say**, Congrats Sir / Mam, please keep this chocolate as an award.

Say – In this game, there was a chance that you may get a 6 or you may not get it however all my customers don't want to leave their financial goals like child education, marriage, retirement, wealth creation, standard of living etc. on chance. I believe that you would also not like to leave these goals on chance.

Say - My role is to ensure that no important goal is left on chance and it's fulfilled in every situation like death, disability, accident, critical illness etc. of the main bread earner.

Power Phrase: Best time to buy life insurance is one day before your death but the irony is no one knows that day.

CHAPTER FORTY-EIGHT

PAPER FOLD ACTIVITY

This activity can be done both online and offline mode anytime as you feel appropriate.

Ask prospect (who need to be the main bread earner of the family) to take a plain sheet of paper preferably A4 size. Ask him / her to draw a small circle in the middle of the paper and write his / her name in this circle. Ask prospect to draw 4 similar circles in the 4 corners of the paper and connect them with 4 straight lines with central circle. See the picture given in the next page.

Now request prospect to write 4 long term (10 Years and above tenure) financial goals which are linked to his / her family and write it with family member names e.g., Khyati's Higher education goal, Himanya's marriage goal, Villa for family and Retirement for wife Jyoti.

Help your prospect to write similar goals in 4 circles. Once s/he completes this exercise, ask him / her to describe about these goals and how important are these goals for him.

Listen with complete attention, interest and body language. Appreciate where so ever you feel right. Now ask prospect to single fold the paper that empty side comes outside and written side is hidden. Now ask prospect to double fold the paper.

Now request prospect to tear away the corner of the paper where his / her name was written. Just indicate that side. You can find out that side by your observation skills. Ask prospect to open all folds of paper. When prospect opens the paper, s / he finds that only his / her name is gone but rest all goals are very much there.

Ask prospect what does this mean to you? Wait for few seconds for the response. Listen to it and do nodding if required. Don't add anything from your side like your own family details etc. Let's prospect feel it, sometime s/he may not express it but you will get signal that message is delivered.

Most of your prospect will get the message, if few of them don't get it then say; **dear prospect; God forbid, if tomorrow you are not there as every day few people die and you can be one of them, this hole shows that only.** If you see further, you will find that somebody need to fulfil financial goals for the family which you have written as there is no change in those goals.

My role as insurance professional is that I help you to plan sufficient insurance so that Life Insurance Company can fill this hole in invisible way and your family can achieve all those goals the way you planned for them.

Explain the product and it's benefits. Link these benefits to various long term goals.

Power Phrase: The only thing a person can buy on the instalment plan, on which his/her spouse won't have to finish the payments after s/he dies, is life insurance.

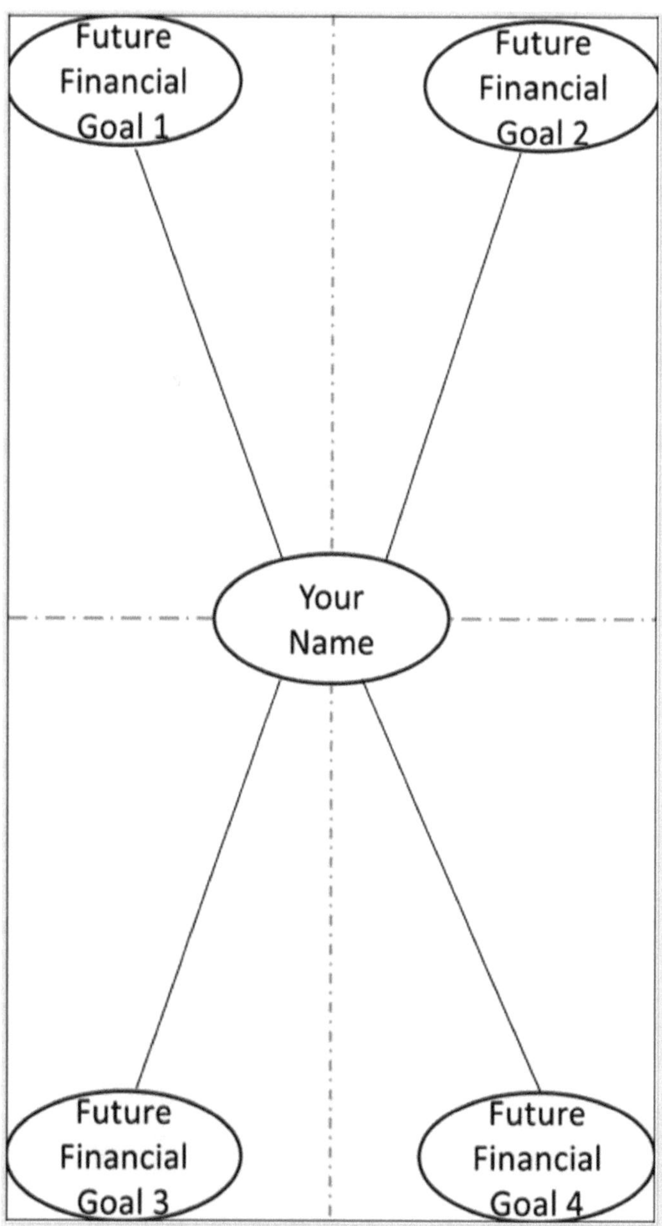

Paper Fold Activity

CHAPTER FORTY-NINE

LOCKS

Carry 2 locks (1 cheap and 1 expensive) with you and show it to the prospects

Ask - What is the first word which comes to your mind by looking at these locks? Drive: protection / safety / theft.

Ask - If you need to go out of your home / office / shop and you have to buy a lock for it, which lock you will buy and why? Drive – A better good quality lock to safeguard home / office / shop even though it may be expensive than the first one.

Ask – For which purposes, you will buy a cheaper lock? Drive – For anything which is not much valuable like drawer within office / home.

Say - My role is to provide appropriate locks in the form of life insurance. I assist people to protect their financial goals like child education, marriage, retirement planning, wealth creation, standard of living etc. and I have all type of locks in form of solutions to cater these financial goals.

Ask - Have you protected all your financial goals?

Power Phrase: You don't buy Life Insurance because you are going to die, but because those you love are going to live.

CHAPTER FIFTY

SURVEY ON CUSTOMER SERVICES

Do this survey only with existing customers. You can do this through face to face, audio, or video call.

Say - Dear Customer, I am conducting a survey on the services provided by my company and me. It will hardly take 2 minutes. We just require your views on the same. With your permission, may I start?

Ask the following questions one by one (you can use printed format, google forms, monkey survey etc. for the same provided by your company or created by you – add customer name on top of it):

1. On a scale of 1-10 where 1 is lowest and 10 is highest, what is your satisfaction level towards the services provided by our company?
2. On a scale of 1-10 where is lowest and 10 is highest, what is your satisfaction level towards services provided by me?
3. On a scale of 1-10 where is lowest and 10 is highest, would you like to refer our company, our products / our services or our name to other people known to you?
4. Please share your suggestions / feedback in any of the areas to provide you better experience / services in future.

Keep noting the responses shared by the customer. If customer is giving any score in between 8 to 10 then it's good score and you can ask for references or repeat business. If customer gives you less than 8 in any of the parameters, you can ask reasons for the same to improve on that area in future.

Say your sincere thanks to the customer for his time and views at the end of the survey.

Power Phrase: When you die and you will, there will be 2 types of lines outside your home. 1 line will be of creditors who gave you credit and many people will be standing in this line to get the money from your family. No one may come forward for 2nd line of debtors except for life insurance seller and this person can handle all creditors of 1st line easily.

CHAPTER FIFTY-ONE

THANK YOU LETTER

Write a letter yourself if your handwriting is good else take help of your family member, friends, colleague, professionals OR type it in a computer and take a colour print out for every existing customer who bought policy from you in the last financial / calendar year or last quarter / last month etc.

Sample Format for Customised Thank You Letter:

Hello Mr / Ms..... I am feeling happy to share that because of your support, we have created History by doing our highest ever business in past one year / last 3 months / last month despite of many challenges.

There have been two important reasons for the same:

1. I have worked on My Knowledge and expertise by getting Certification courses from (mention your company name and other organizations from where you learnt new things) and have learned all aspects of financial planning based on which I could help our clients to do their financial planning.

2. Secondly our clients, who have got an insight about the need of financial planning in their lives and took the decision of buying term, retirement, saving plans and guaranteed plans etc from us.

Please accept my sincere thanks for taking this decision and going ahead with us. I promise that I will continue to serve you with best financial planning tools in future as well and will keep doing reviews time to time.

I am praying for good health for you and your family. See you soon.

Regards,

Your Signature

Your Name

Power Phrase: Every seller on this earth earns some profits by selling any product or service. So you will not buy life insurance as somebody said no to you for giving back the commission part or not offering discount. Whose loss is this?

Disclaimer

To protect the privacy of certain individuals the names and identifying details have been changed. This is a work of fiction. Any names or characters, businesses or places, events or incidents, are fictitious. Any resemblance to actual persons, living or dead, or actual events is purely coincidental.

It is notified that neither the content provider nor the editor or any person related with this book in any manner shall be responsible for any damage or loss of action to anyone, of any kind, in any manner, therefrom.

How To Contact The Author!

First of all, please accept my sincere thanks for investing your time to read this book.

If you like it, do share about this book to others. Gift this book to others.

If you have any feedback, views to share with the author then the author can be approached through the following mail id: _failthefailure2@gmail.com_

You can contact through the same mail id for any inquiry on content development, training delivery, fire walk activity or motivational speech.

Once again, thank you so much for being part of my journey.

Lots of blessings and love.

From: Harbans Lal Arora